Philip Neri
The Laughing Saint

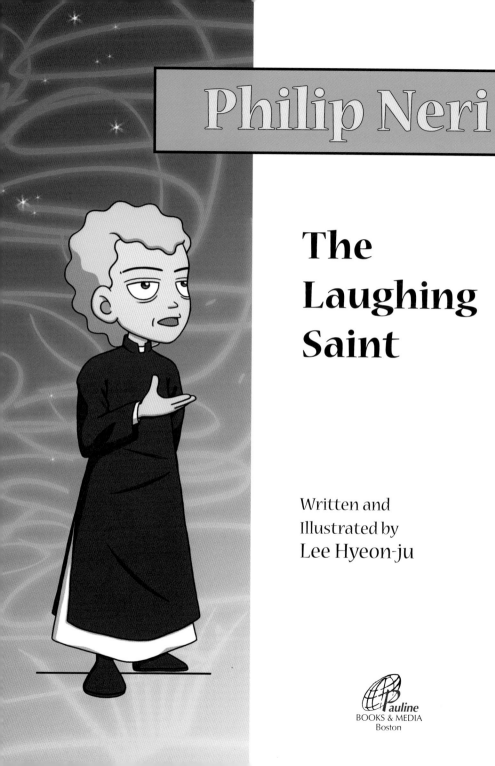

Philip Neri

The Laughing Saint

Written and
Illustrated by
Lee Hyeon-ju

Pauline
BOOKS & MEDIA
Boston

Library of Congress Cataloging-in-Publication Data

Yi, Hyon-ju (Cartoonist)
 [Myongnang han songin P'illippo Neri. English]
 Philip Neri, the laughing saint / by Lee Hyeon-ju ; translated by Kate Yoon.
    pages cm
 ISBN 978-0-8198-6008-8 -- ISBN 0-8198-6008-5
 1. Neri, Filippo, Saint, 1515-1595--Comic books, strips, etc. 2. Christian saints--Italy--
Biography--Comic books, strips, etc. 3. Graphic novels. I. Title.
  BX4700.F33Y513 2014
  282.092--dc23
  [B]
                        2014012802

The Scripture quotations contained herein are from the *New Revised Standard Version Bible: Catholic Edition*, copyright © 1989, 1993, Division of Christian Education of the National Council of the Churches of Christ in the United States of America. Used by permission. All rights reserved.

Translated by Kate Yoon.

명랑한 성인 필립보 네리 (Philip Neri, the Cheerful Saint) © 2012

by LEE Hyeon-ju, www.pauline.or.kr.

Originally published by Pauline Books & Media, Seoul, Korea. All rights reserved.

Copyright © 2014, Daughters of St. Paul for English edition

Published by Pauline Books & Media, 50 Saint Pauls Avenue, Boston, MA 02130–3491

Printed in the U.S.A.

PNTLS VSAUSAPEOILL7-2710185 6008-5

www.pauline.org

Pauline Books & Media is the publishing house of the Daughters of St. Paul, an international congregation of women religious serving the Church with the communications media.

3 4 5 6 7 8 9 10   25 24 23 22 21

SCHOOL AT A DOMINICAN* MONASTERY IN SAN MARCO

*DOMINICANS ARE A RELIGIOUS ORDER OF PRIESTS FOUNDED BY SAINT DOMINIC.

PHILIP, CAN YOU TRANSLATE THIS LATIN FOR ME?

NO . . .

WHAAAT? STOP BEING SUCH A SNOB AND JUST DO IT.

NOOOOOOO! I FORGOT! THEY'RE ALL GONE!

NO WAY! LATIN IS YOUR BEST SUBJECT. HOW COULD YOU FORGET EVERY WORD?

WAAAH!

2

I'M NOT TALKING ABOUT LATIN. I'M TALKING ABOUT BANANAS. THE BANANAS ARE ALL GONE. I ATE THEM ALL!

PILE OF BANANA PEELS
⬇

BANANAS?

NOT LATIN?

NOPE!

SNORT

P-H-I-L-I-P!!!

ESCAPES

PHILIP NERI!!!

CUT THE JOKES! WHEN ARE YOU GOING TO GET YOURSELF TOGETHER AND GROW UP?

I'M NOT GOING TO GET *MYSELF* TOGETHER; I'M GOING TO GET MY *FOOD* TOGETHER.

HAHAHA, LOOKS LIKE PHILIP IS AT IT AGAIN. HE'S SUCH A TERRIBLE JOKESTER!

BUT HIS HUMOR IS CONTAGIOUS; HE'S ALSO SMART AND KIND. AND LET'S NOT FORGET HOW FAITHFUL HE IS. . . .

IN FACT, I THINK HE'D MAKE A GREAT PRIEST SOMEDAY. I MEAN, THIS KID ATTRACTS PEOPLE . . .

PHI-LIP!

HAHAHA

하 하

하 하

HEE HEE

5

STEPMOMMY . . .

PHILIP . . .

STEPMOMMY!

P-H-I-L-I-P!

6

A FEW DAYS LATER . . .

QUACK!
PLUNK!

SOMEONE SAID THAT YOU'RE GOING TO SAN GERMANO SO YOU CAN BE A MERCHANT. THAT DOESN'T SOUND RIGHT . . .

SORRY DUCK . . .

QUACK

QUACK

FLUTTER

FLUTTER

WHAT IF I SAID I WAS GOING TO BE A BUSINESSMAN AND NOT A MERCHANT? DOES THAT SOUND BETTER?

WHY A MERCHANT? I THOUGHT YOU'D BECOME A PRIEST. YOU'RE SO GOOD IN LATIN AND YOU ENJOY READING THE PSALMS AND YOU PRAY A LOT.

12

IN 1532, THE MEDICI FAMILY RETURNED TO FLORENCE AFTER A TIME OF EXILE. THEY WERE POLITICALLY POWERFUL AND WEALTHY AND RULED THE CITY. SINCE PHILIP'S FATHER HAD OPPOSED THE MEDICIS, THERE WERE FEW OPPORTUNITIES FOR PHILIP'S FAMILY IN FLORENCE.

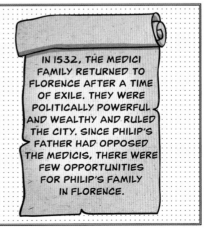

I'M MOVING SOUTH TO LIVE WITH UNCLE ROMOLO. FROM HIM I'LL LEARN HOW TO BECOME A WEALTHY BUSINESSMAN. I'LL BE A MILLIONAIRE!

FINE!

UMM . . . PHILIP . . . WE CAN STILL BE FRIENDS FOREVER, RIGHT?!

WHAT ABOUT YOU?

QUAAAACK
DHOH~♥

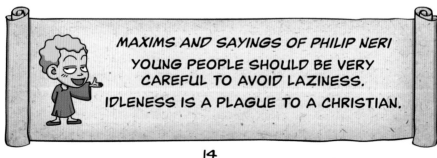

MAXIMS AND SAYINGS OF PHILIP NERI

YOUNG PEOPLE SHOULD BE VERY CAREFUL TO AVOID LAZINESS.

IDLENESS IS A PLAGUE TO A CHRISTIAN.

BUT SOON PHILIP REALIZED THAT BEING WEALTHY DIDN'T MATTER TO HIM.

MASTER PHILIP! YOU'RE GONNA GET HURT!

PHILIP, PHILIP!

핍보 —
핍보 —

AGAIN?

HEY, HAVE YOU SEEN PHILIP?

HE WENT TO THE MONASTERY.

16

MONTE CASSINO
MONASTERY

YOU LOOK LOST IN THOUGHT. WHAT ARE YOU THINKING ABOUT?

OH, A MONK!

APPROACHES

I DON'T UNDERSTAND WHY YOU'RE ALL WEARING RAGS. I'VE DONATED LOTS OF MONEY TO THE MONKS. WHAT'S GOING ON?!

DO YOU WANT TO LOOK LIKE BEGGARS?

THESE CLOTHES STILL HAVE LOTS OF LIFE LEFT IN THEM.

BRUSH

17

FATHER, I'LL GIVE YOU ANOTHER DONATION FOR THE POOR PEOPLE, THEN.

HAHAHA! YOU'RE SO GENEROUS AND WARM-HEARTED, PHILIP.

HERE, PHILIP, I'LL GIVE YOU A GIFT TOO. GO AND READ GOD'S WORDS.

BYE!

WHERE DID HE HAVE THIS BIBLE HIDDEN?

FLIP FLIP FLIP

JESUS, LOOKING AT HIM, LOVED HIM AND SAID, "YOU LACK ONE THING; GO, SELL WHAT YOU OWN, AND GIVE THE MONEY TO THE POOR, AND YOU WILL HAVE TREASURE IN HEAVEN; THEN COME, FOLLOW ME." (MARK 10:21)

MASTER PHILIP, YOU'LL GET SICK IF YOU KEEP WORKING LIKE THIS.

WHEN I FINISH THEN I CAN GET SICK.

BAA (매애~)

BAA (매애~)

BAA (매애~)

PHILIP, IF YOU LISTEN TO ME, YOU'LL MAKE INTEREST ON YOUR MONEY.

UMM . . . OK.

JESUS, LOOKING AT HIM, LOVED HIM AND SAID, "YOU LACK ONE THING; GO, SELL WHAT YOU OWN, AND GIVE THE MONEY TO THE POOR, AND YOU WILL HAVE TREASURE IN HEAVEN; THEN COME, FOLLOW ME." (MARK 10:21)

DESPITE ALL THAT UNCLE ROMOLO WAS TEACHING PHILIP ABOUT MAKING MONEY, PHILIP FELT DRAWN TO TAKING CARE OF THE POOR THE WAY THE MONKS DID.

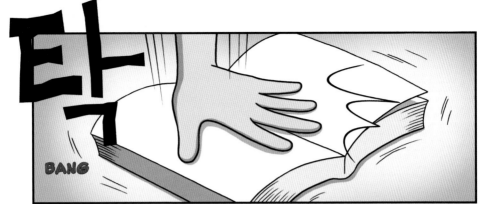

BANG

UNCLE ROMOLO . . .

PHILIP, I'M GLAD YOU'RE HERE. LET'S GO OUT TODAY.

I HAVE SOMETHING TO TELL YOU.

WHAT IS IT?

I . . .

I'VE DECIDED TO GO TO ROME, UNCLE.

FOR A VISIT?
(HMM . . .
THAT DOESN'T
SEEM RIGHT.)

NO, NOT
A VISIT!

FAINT

UNCLE!

PHILIP,
WHY ARE
YOU
DOING
THIS?

ARE THE MONKS
FROM MONTE
CASSINO MAKING
YOU DO THIS?

ARE THEY
TRYING TO
FORCE YOU
TO BECOME
ONE OF
THEM?

I'M NOT GOING
TO ROME SO I
CAN BE A
PRIEST.

I DON'T WANT TO
LEAVE YOU ALONE,
BUT I WANT TO
FOLLOW GOD'S
CALLING. I WANT TO
STUDY RELIGION AND
PHILOSOPHY IN ROME
SO I CAN HELP THE
POOR AND SICK TO
KNOW GOD.

YOUR UNCLE IS GIVING YOU THIS PLACE AS A GIFT.

헉!

WHAT'S WRONG? IS IT TOO SMALL?

WELL . . .

NO!!!

꼬아―!

ONE SMALL ROOM.

달랑 한 칸

AHH, ROOM SWEET ROOM!

난 이곳에 만족!

PHILIP WANTED TO LIVE SIMPLY, SO HE CHOSE TO LIVE IN ONE ROOM.

HERE, TAKE THIS MONEY. I SOLD THE HOUSE MY UNCLE BOUGHT ME.

PLEASE DON'T DO THIS. YOUR UNCLE WILL BE SO ANGRY.

25

PLEASE TAKE THIS AND DONATE IT IN MY UNCLE'S NAME TO HELP THE POOR IN SAN GERMANO.

ALSO, I DON'T NEED A SERVANT SO YOU CAN RETURN HOME.

OH, I CAN'T DO THAT.

I HAVE A LITTLE BAG OF MONEY FOR YOU AS WELL . . .

REALLY?!

PHILIP AGREED TO TUTOR THE CHILDREN OF A FAMILY FROM FLORENCE LIVING IN ROME IN EXCHANGE FOR A ROOM IN THEIR HOME.

PHEW! LOOKS LIKE I'M JUST ABOUT DONE ORGANIZING EVERYTHING.

CLAP CLAP

MY NEW LIFE HAS JUST BEGUN!

26

SAPIENZA UNIVERSITY, 1537

IS GOD *EVER* FAIR?

WHAT?! YOU STUDY THEOLOGY HERE. HOW CAN YOU ASK THAT?

I THINK *GOD IS UNFAIR* BECAUSE SOMEBODY SPENDS 8 TO 10 HOURS PRAYING *AND* HE STILL GETS BETTER GRADES THAN ANYONE ELSE IN PHILOSOPHY AND THEOLOGY!

DO YOU MEAN PHILIP?

YEAH, IN THE TWO YEARS WE'VE KNOWN PHILIP I'VE FIGURED OUT HE MUST BE A GENIUS OR SOMETHING.

YOU'RE RIGHT. I GET SO JEALOUS OF HIM. HE'S SMART AND LIKABLE. AND I'M PRETTY SURE HE'D MAKE A GREAT PRIEST. THERE'S JUST ONE THING . . . HE'S TOO MISCHIEVOUS—

BOO!

28

29

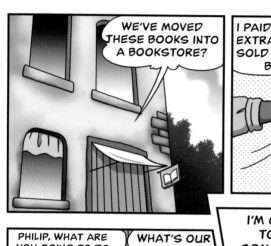

WHAAAT? WHAT IS THIS BUILDING? YOU'RE NOT BUYING IT, RIGHT?

THIS NEIGHBORHOOD IS TERRIBLE.

DON'T HESITATE, COME ON IN!

I AM NOT HESITATING. I DON'T WANT TO GO.

GAG

I TOLD YOU SOMETHING WAS FISHY.

I KNEW PHILIP WAS UP TO SOMETHING.

I KNOW IT'S NOT MUCH, BUT YOU'LL BE ABLE TO BUY SOME BREAD AND MEDICINE.

YOU SHOULDN'T KEEP DOING THIS FOR US.

I AM NOT GIVING THIS TO YOU. GOD IS GIVING IT TO YOU.

GOD?

YES, MA'AM, THIS IS MONEY FROM GOD. I'M ONLY THE DELIVERY PERSON.

THANK YOU. THANK YOU, GOD! MAY GOD BLESS YOU, YOUNG MAN.

PLEASE PRAY FOR ME TOO, OK?

HERE . . .

UH . . . I CAN 않아서 즈저 . . . HARDLY REACH.

GRAB

PHILIP NERI! WHAT THE HECK ARE YOU DOING? HAVE YOU LOST YOUR MIND?

YOU SOLD ALL THE BOOKS FOR THESE BEGGARS? HOW ARE YOU GOING TO STUDY AND LIVE WITH NO BOOKS AND NO MONEY?

WHAT? YOU CALLED US BEGGARS? THAT WASN'T VERY NICE.

OH, MY! HE SOLD HIS BOOKS TO HELP US?

I JUST THOUGHT HE WAS RICH.

HE DOESN'T LOOK RICH.

DON'T FORGET ABOUT ME. I NEED MONEY TOO.

PLEASE DON'T WORRY. MY UNCLE IS SUPPORTING ME FINANCIALLY. NOW, LET'S GO TO THE OTHER SIDE OF THE ROOM TO TALK. YOU'RE HURTING THEIR FEELINGS.

WHAT AM I GOING TO DO WITH YOU, PHILIP?

33

UNCLE?

WHAT HAVE YOU DONE WITH ALL THE MONEY I SEND YOU EVERY MONTH? YOU LIVE IN A SMALL ROOM INSTEAD OF A NICE HOUSE. AND, WHAT'S WITH YOUR CLOTHES? YOU LOOK LIKE A BEGGAR!

IN FACT, I BET WHEN BEGGARS SEE YOU, THEY PITY YOU AND GIVE YOU MONEY.

MESSY

DIRTY

후줄근

TORN

WELL, WHEN I DON'T HAVE ANY MORE MONEY I DO BEG SOMETIMES.

WHAT? I SEND YOU PLENTY OF MONEY. YOU SHOULDN'T NEED TO BEG.

YOU HAVEN'T SEEN ME IN OVER TWO YEARS, DO YOU REALLY WANT TO SCOLD ME?

IT'S TRUE, I'VE COME A GOOD DISTANCE TO SEE HIM, I CAN'T JUST SCOLD HIM . . .

I'LL KNOCK SOME SENSE INTO HIM!

NOOOOOOO!

으악

SCREECH

NICE TO MEET YOU . . .

MASTER PHILIP.

WHO . . .

IS THIS?

UMM . . . YOU TOLD ME TO COME WITH HER. SHE'S . . .

WELL . . .

YOU SEE . . .

AH! NICE TO MEET YOU. MY NAME IS PHILIP.

I'VE HEARD A LOT ABOUT YOU FROM ROMOLO.

UNCLE, HAVE YOU KNOWN HER LONG? IS SHE A NEW LOVE?

38

PLEASE HAVE SOME TEA.

I HAD A HUGE PARTY FOR MY FRIENDS AND I DON'T HAVE ANY FOOD TO OFFER YOU.

YEAH, "PARTY"–RIGHT. YOU'RE ALWAYS JOKING, PHILIP. YOU PROBABLY GAVE ALL YOUR FOOD TO THE HOMELESS.

WE'RE FINE WITH JUST THE TEA.

GRR

AWW . . . JUST LOOK AT HIS FACE.

SHY

BLUSH

GREAT! THEY GET ALONG.

아저씨가 왕박사래 이때가 맛있는 거 실컷 얻어먹어요~

ROLLS EYES

아주 죽이 착착

그래요. 좋을 생각이에요.

맞는구먼!

PHILIP!

OUT WITH IT, YOUNG MAN. WHY DO YOU LIVE IN THIS ONE LITTLE ROOM INSTEAD OF THE NICE BIG HOUSE I BOUGHT YOU? WHAT'S THE REAL REASON?

UNCLE, YOU'VE GIVEN ME SO MUCH AND I APPRECIATE IT. BUT THAT HOUSE WAS JUST TOO BIG FOR ME. I LIKE THIS ROOM. I CAN FOCUS ON MY STUDIES AND IT'S NOT TOO FAR FROM SCHOOL. AND IT'S CLOSE TO THE POOR PEOPLE GOD IS ASKING ME TO CARE FOR.

BUT WHY CAN'T YOU LIVE IN A NICE BIG HOUSE . . .

AND BRING THE POOR THERE TO HELP THEM? DO YOU REALLY NEED TO LIVE *HERE*?

WOW! YOU'RE SO SMART. WHY DIDN'T I THINK OF THAT?

YOU'RE **THE BEST!**

STOP JOKING AROUND!

UNCLE, I'M TRYING TO FOLLOW GOD'S PATH AND LIVE BY HIS TEACHINGS. AS SIMPLY AS I LIVE HERE, IT IS STILL BETTER THAN THE LIVES OF THE POOR PEOPLE OUT THERE.

CLAP

CLAP

CLAP

CLAP

HE'S AWESOME!

DON'T WORRY ABOUT ME. I'M STUDYING HARD AND GETTING GOOD GRADES. I'M JUST TRYING TO LIVE AS GOD WANTS.

WELL... YOU'VE REALLY GROWN UP.

NODS

41

WELL, LET'S . . .

...HAVE FUN TODAY. MY RICH UNCLE IS IN TOWN. WE SHOULD EAT TILL OUR STOMACHS POP!

WHAT?!

WHAT A GREAT IDEA!

PHILIP, WHEN ARE YOU GOING TO STOP JOKING AROUND?

LET'S HURRY. I KNOW ALL THE GREAT RESTAURANTS IN ROME. YOU'LL HAVE TO TRY THIS GOURMET ROMAN BEEF . . . SO DELICIOUS!!

I'LL TRY SOME OF THAT ! THIS IS EXCITING!

MAXIMS AND SAYINGS OF PHILIP NERI

IN GIVING ALMS TO THE POOR, WE MUST ACT AS GOOD MINISTERS OF THE PROVIDENCE OF GOD.

I TRIED SUPPORTING HIM FINANCIALLY, BUT HE USED ALL THE MONEY I GAVE HIM TO HELP THE HOMELESS AND BEGGARS.

HE'S SO POOR AND LOOKS HOMELESS HIMSELF. BUT HE SAYS HE'S HAPPY BECAUSE HE IS RICH IN OTHER WAYS.

HE ATE ENOUGH MEAT FOR FIFTEEN PEOPLE. I BET HE HADN'T EATEN FOR A LONG TIME.

DIRTY 지글지글 MESSY 후줄 후줄

I KNEW YOU WEREN'T HAPPY TO SPEND ALL THAT MONEY FOR OUR OUTING.

HOW WILL ANYONE KNOW ABOUT THE GOOD WORK HE'S DOING IF HE CONTINUES TO LIVE LIKE THAT?

HAHAHA

IT'S NOT LIKE PHILIP IS SPECIAL OR UNIQUE ALL OF A SUDDEN. HE'S ALWAYS BEEN CONCERNED FOR OTHERS.

LATER IN ROME AT SAPIENZA COLLEGE . . .

COULD YOU REPEAT THAT ONE MORE TIME?

I WANT TO QUIT SCHOOL. I HAVE LOTS OF WORK TO DO.

MR. NERI, YOU HAVE A BRIGHT FUTURE. YOU'RE SMART AND COULD BECOME A GREAT PHILOSOPHER OR THEOLOGIAN.

YOU'LL REGRET QUITTING.

I'LL REGRET IT MORE IF I DON'T.

CAN YOU EXPLAIN *WHY YOU WANT TO QUIT?*

IT'S SIMPLE. I'VE LEARNED ENOUGH TO BEGIN WHAT GOD WANTS ME TO DO. THERE'S NO REASON FOR ME TO STAY— IT'S TIME FOR ME TO START DOING GOOD DEEDS.

MAY GOD BLESS YOU.

꾸벅

BOW

WHAT DID HE SAY? I CAN'T BELIEVE HE'S LEAVING.

CLOSE

탁

PHILIP, IS IT TRUE? ARE YOU QUITTING?

YOU GOT SOMETHING BETTER TO DO THAN STUDY?

WORD SURE DOES TRAVEL FAST.

PHILIP?

IS THAT MY BOOK?

YOU DON'T HAVE TO QUIT SCHOOL. YOU CAN STILL DO GOOD DEEDS WHILE YOU STUDY.

YOU'RE RIGHT, BUT I BELIEVE GOD WANTS ME TO DEVOTE MYSELF TO GROWING IN HOLINESS AND TO SERVING MY NEIGHBOR.

GO FOR IT!

I'VE COME TO REALIZE THAT GOD IS ASKING ME TO TEACH THE POOR AND UNEDUCATED. THEY HAVEN'T HAD THE OPPORTUNITY TO KNOW GOD. I NEED TO START NOW.

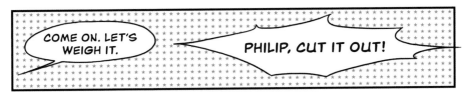

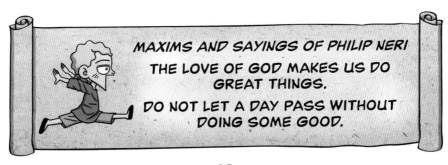

MAXIMS AND SAYINGS OF PHILIP NERI

THE LOVE OF GOD MAKES US DO GREAT THINGS.

DO NOT LET A DAY PASS WITHOUT DOING SOME GOOD.

THE REFORMATION BEGAN IN 1513. IT CAUSED A LOT OF PEOPLE TO QUESTION HOW CATHOLIC LEADERS HAD USED THEIR AUTHORITY. MANY PEOPLE NO LONGER TRUSTED THEM. THEY LEFT THE CATHOLIC CHURCH AND JOINED NEW DENOMINATIONS. THE CHURCH WAS SITTING ON A BARREL OF GUNPOWDER AND WAS FACING A CRISIS.

ALTHOUGH THERE HAD BEEN RELIGIOUS REFORMATION IN THE CHURCH BEFORE, THIS CRISIS WAS VERY DEEP. BECAUSE PEOPLE ON BOTH SIDES WERE TOO STUBBORN, THE CHURCH WAS DIVIDED.

WE NEED REFORM!

NOT THE WAY YOU WANT IT!

POPE PAUL III WAS AT THE CENTER OF THE REFORMATION CRISIS.

IN 1539, ONCE POPE PAUL III WAS INSTALLED AS THE CHURCH'S LEADER, HE TRIED VERY HARD TO SETTLE THE CONFLICTS BETWEEN COUNTRIES AND WORKED TO DEAL WITH ISLAM'S PRESENCE IN EUROPE.

GENERALLY, WHEN A CAPTAIN TRIES TO SUDDENLY CHANGE THE DIRECTION OF A BIG SHIP, IT CAN EASILY FLIP. THE CATHOLIC CHURCH WAS LIKE A VERY BIG SHIP AT SEA. POPE PAUL III CALLED THE COUNCIL OF TRENT IN 1545 TO ADDRESS THE ISSUES THAT THE PROTESTANT REFORMERS RAISED.

THE COUNCIL OF TRENT ALSO TRIED TO RESTORE UNITY IN THE CHURCH AND KEEP IT FROM BREAKING FURTHER APART. BUT EVERY GREAT CAPTAIN NEEDS A LOYAL CREW.

I WAS PART OF THE LOYAL CREW. I ALSO WANTED TO DO WHAT I COULD TO HELP THE CHURCH SAIL IN THE RIGHT DIRECTION.

A LONG TIME AGO . . . THERE WAS A SAINT CALLED CHRISTOPHER.

LET ME TELL YOU GUYS ABOUT HIM.

I NEED TO LISTEN TO HIM CAREFULLY. HE WILL BUY ME DINNER AFTER THIS.

BUT JUST TEACHING THE POOR WAS NOT ENOUGH FOR PHILIP. GOD WAS CALLING HIM TO DO MORE.

54

PHILIP, DO YOU HAVE A SECOND?

MA'AM, YOU HAVE A FEVER.

WHAT'S GOING ON?

FATHER GREGORIO PASSED OUT DUE TO FATIGUE AND . . .

THERE ARE JUST SO MANY PEOPLE WHO NEED HELP. THERE ARE TOO MANY FOR US.

I'VE SEEN ALL THE GOOD *YOU* ARE DOING. THE PEOPLE NEED FOOD AND GUIDANCE, BUT THE REST OF US ARE SO TIRED. IT'S TOO MUCH.

SOME OF US HAVE ALREADY LEFT.

HMM.

AND I ACHE ALL OVER.

YES, OF COURSE.

WHAT AM I EVEN DOING HERE? WHAT'S WRONG WITH ME?

MARTINO.

PAT PAT

I'LL START RIGHT AWAY.

UH-OH, THIS COULD BE A MISTAKE. JUST LOOK AT THE MISCHIEVOUS EXPRESSION ON HIS FACE.

신부님들 모이세요~

LISTEN! EVERYONE, GATHER ROUND.

웅성 CROWDED

CROWDED 웅성

웅성 CROWDED

WHAT'S GOING ON?

DO WE HAVE A MEETING?

HAVE THEY DECIDED WE SHOULD STOP GATHERING LIKE THIS?

AFTER 10 HOURS . . .

WHAT'S GOING ON? ARE WE REALLY GOING TO PRAY FOR 40 HOURS STRAIGHT?!

AFTER 29 HOURS . . .

FAINT

PASS OUT

AFTER 40 HOURS . . .

RING-

A-LING

WE'RE DONE. GOOD PRAYING, EVERYONE!

EXHAUSTED

STRETCH

AIEEEE~

THAT WAS HARD.

MY FEET FELL ASLEEP. I CAN'T STAND UP.

DID YOU NOTICE PHILIP? HE DIDN'T MOVE DURING THE WHOLE 40 HOURS WE PRAYED.

REALLY? I DIDN'T SEE ANYTHING. I THINK I FAINTED.

PHILIP IS REALLY ONE OF A KIND. WITH HIM SHOWING US HOW TO LIVE, I'LL CONTINUE TO FOLLOW THE TEACHINGS OF THE CATHOLIC CHURCH, EVEN THOUGH SOME OF THE PEOPLE IN THE CHURCH DON'T ALWAYS DO THE RIGHT THING.

RING-A-LING

때응~ 때응~

NOW THAT WE ARE DONE PRAYING, WE CAN GO DO GOOD DEEDS.

LET'S GO OUTSIDE!

잠- 잠-

UMM . . .
GUYS?
HELLO?

쿨~~~
ZZZZZZZZZ

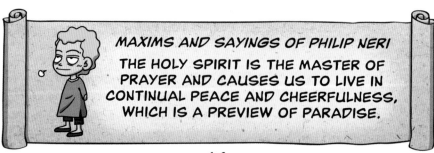

MAXIMS AND SAYINGS OF PHILIP NERI

THE HOLY SPIRIT IS THE MASTER OF
PRAYER AND CAUSES US TO LIVE IN
CONTINUAL PEACE AND CHEERFULNESS,
WHICH IS A PREVIEW OF PARADISE.

WHAT ARE WE GOING TO DO? THERE'S JUST SO MUCH CORRUPTION IN THE CHURCH.

I'VE BECOME DISILLUSIONED. IS GOD STILL WITH THIS CHURCH?

I DON'T THINK I'LL BE GOING TO CHURCH ANYMORE.

WHERE DID THE VIRTUES OF FAITH, HOPE, AND LOVE GO?

LIMP 절뚝

절뚝 LIMP

WHAT'S WRONG WITH HIM?

EXCUSE ME . . .

FATHER . . .

YES, CAN I HELP YOU?

WELL, I'M NOT . . .

BUT. . . I MEAN . . .

I DON'T GO TO CHURCH MUCH, BUT . . .

CAN I HAVE SOME B-B-BREAD?

OF COURSE YOU CAN!

WE DON'T HAVE MUCH, BUT HERE, TAKE THIS. I'M SORRY WE CAN'T GIVE YOU MORE.

OH, NO . . . THIS IS PERFECT. THANK YOU.

STOP RIGHT THERE!

LIMP LIMP

HUH?

WHO? ME?

HEART THUMP

YOU! YOU DON'T GO TO CHURCH, RIGHT? YOU'RE NOT EVEN CATHOLIC, RIGHT?

UM... I... WELL...

HOW DARE YOU COME TO THE CHURCH AND LEAVE RIGHT AFTER GETTING SOME BREAD!

THAT POOR MAN. WHAT IS PHILIP DOING?!

IT LOOKS LIKE PHILIP'S GOING TO BEAT HIM UP.

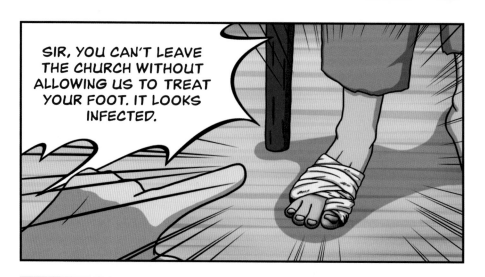

SIR, YOU CAN'T LEAVE THE CHURCH WITHOUT ALLOWING US TO TREAT YOUR FOOT. IT LOOKS INFECTED.

COME ON. WE'RE GOING BACK TO THE CHURCH. IT DOESN'T MATTER IF YOU'RE CATHOLIC OR NOT, WE WANT TO HELP. WHEN WE GET THERE, WE'LL TAKE CARE OF YOUR FOOT.

YOU'RE GOING TO BREAK MY NECK IF YOU KEEP DRAGGING ME LIKE THIS.

HAHA. LOOK AT FATHER* PHILIP, DRAGGING IN ONE OF HIS LAMBS.

WHETHER HE KNOWS IT OR NOT, THAT GUY WILL GROW CLOSER TO GOD BECAUSE OF FATHER PHILIP'S PRAYERS.

SHOCK!

*ALTHOUGH PHILIP WAS NOT YET A PRIEST, HE WAS KNOWN BY MANY OF THE PEOPLE AS "FATHER" PHILIP.

WOW! SEEING THE LOVE WITH WHICH FATHER PHILIP IS TAKING CARE OF THAT MAN IS AMAZING.

SEE? GOD HASN'T ABANDONED THE CATHOLIC CHURCH! THANK YOU, LORD!

HEY!

DIDN'T YOU JUST SAY YOU WERE GOING TO LEAVE THE CHURCH?

HEY, EVERYONE, DON'T BE SHY! GATHER 'ROUND.

I'M TOO EMBARRASSED TO GET TOO CLOSE.

SO WHAT IF I DID?! CAN'T A PERSON CHANGE HIS MIND?!

OK, CALM DOWN!

A SMILE CAN BE SUCH A BLESSING TO ALL WE MEET.

COME ON, EVERYONE—SMILE!

LET'S SMILE TOGETHER!

CLAP

CLAP

OH, BROTHER! NOW NO ONE WILL BE ABLE TO STOP HIM.

WHY WOULD YOU WANT TO? HE'S POPULAR BECAUSE HE'S SO CHEERFUL AND FUNNY.

YEAH, FATHER PHILIP TREATED MY SHOULDER AND PRAYED FOR ME. NOW THE PAIN'S GONE.

HE'S AMAZING. HE TREATS EVERYONE THE SAME, WHETHER THEY'RE POOR OR RICH.

YOU'RE RIGHT. HE'S DIFFERENT FROM PRIESTS WHO ARE SUPER-SERI-OUS AND CAN BE DIFFICULT TO TALK TO. WE'RE BLESSED TO HAVE FATHER PHILIP.

HEY, STOP CALLING HIM FATHER. HE'S NOT A REAL PRIEST.

PINCH

PHILIP HASN'T BEEN ORDAINED A PRIEST. FATHER MARTINO, ON THE OTHER HAND, IS A REAL PRIEST BECAUSE HE HAS BEEN ORDAINED.

OH, SHOULD I STOP CALLING HIM "FATHER" THEN?

WHAT WILL YOU CALL HIM IF YOU DON'T CALL HIM "FATHER"?

DON'T SAY IT. DON'T SAY IT.

I DON'T KNOW. I GUESS AS LONG AS I DON'T CALL HIM LATE TO SUPPER . . .

ARRRR! I JUST KNEW YOU WERE GOING TO MAKE A LAME JOKE!

HAHA!

SOME TIME LATER . . .

PHILIP!

71

WHAT? YOU'RE PRAYING AGAIN? AREN'T YOU EXHAUSTED?

I'M TALKING TO GOD ABOUT SOME OF THE PEOPLE WHO WERE GOOFING AROUND DURING PRAYER TIME.

I WILL NOT FEEL GUILTY.

LISTEN, PHILIP, IT'S TIME TO STOP PRAYING AND TIME FOR YOU TO REST! IF YOU KEEP WORKING THIS HARD, YOU'LL DIE OF EXHAUSTION.

I'M OK. DON'T WORRY ABOUT ME. I'VE ALREADY BOOKED THE DATE WITH GOD— MAY 26, 1595. I'LL STOP PRAYING NOW.

THAT'S STILL A LONG WAY OFF. WHAT HAPPENS THAT DAY?

THAT'S THE DAY I'LL SEE GOD FACE-TO-FACE.

YOU'RE JOKING, RIGHT?

DO YOU WANT ME TO FIND OUT WHAT YOUR DAY WILL BE TOO? JUST LOOK ME IN THE EYES.

WHATEVER! JUST FORGET IT. I DON'T CARE WHETHER YOU LIVE OR DIE.

BUT YOU *DO* CARE. THAT'S WHY YOU CAME TO CHECK UP ON ME!

OㅏㅡOH!

ㅊㅏㅡ

YEAH, NOW I REMEMBER...

BECAUSE OF ALL YOUR JOKES I ALMOST FORGOT WHY I CAME.

MARTINO, HOW SWEET!

마티~ 나 가뜩이넘었어~

PHILIP, FATHER PERSIANO WOULD LIKE TO SEE YOU RIGHT AWAY.

73

74

COME IN, FATHER PHILIP.

YOU DON'T HAVE TO CALL ME FATHER, FATHER.

HAHAHA! PLEASE SIT DOWN.

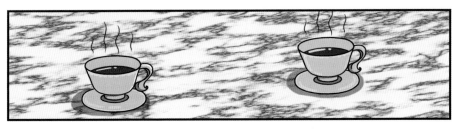

PHILIP, IT'S TIME FOR YOU TO SERIOUSLY THINK ABOUT BECOMING A PRIEST.

FATHER, IS EVERY-THING OK? FATHER MARTINO MADE IT SOUND URGENT.

AS I VOLUNTEER, I AM ALSO LEARNING FROM THE PEOPLE. GOD WANTS ME TO BE HUMBLE AND LEARN FROM OTHERS—IT WAS A DUTY GIVEN TO ME BY GOD AT BIRTH.

YOU CAN BE HUMBLE AND BE A PRIEST. IF YOU BECOME A PRIEST, YOU'LL STILL BE ABLE TO DO GOOD. THE PEOPLE WILL TRUST YOU EVEN MORE WITH THEIR SOULS.

IF I BECOME A PRIEST, PEOPLE WILL POINT AT ME AND SHOUT, "THERE GOES THE BEGGAR PRIEST!"

PLEASE, PHILIP! THINK ABOUT IT ONE MORE TIME.

NO THANKS!

ON MAY 23, 1551, AT SANTO TOMMASO CHURCH IN PARIONE . . .

MY LORD AND MY GOD . . .

I WANT TO BECOME A PRIEST TO SERVE YOU AND HELP YOUR PEOPLE.

AFTER HIS ORDINATION, PHILIP WAS ASSIGNED TO SAN GIROLAMO IN ROME.

FOOTSTEPS

HELLO, MY SISTER. WOULD YOU LIKE ME TO HEAR YOUR CONFESSION?

WHAT?

MY "SPECIALTY" IS HEARING CONFESSION. I'M REALLY GOOD AT IT.

HAHAHA! YOU'RE FUNNY. I'LL ASK YOU SOMETIME IN THE FUTURE TO HEAR IT.

I'LL TAKE THAT AS A PROMISE! I'LL SEE YOU NEXT TIME FOR SURE.

THERE YOU GO AGAIN. STOP BEGGING PEOPLE FOR CONFESSIONS. WHY DO YOU DO THAT?

THE SACRAMENT OF CONFESSION BRINGS PEOPLE BACK TO GOD. IT'S SO IMPORTANT!

IMAGINE . . .

82

CONFESSION ROOM

SNIFFLE

ONE DAY, SOMEONE COMES TO CHURCH FOR CONFESSION, BUT GOES AWAY SAD BECAUSE THERE'S NO PRIEST WHO MAKES HIMSELF AVAILABLE TO LISTEN.

THAT PERSON CAME BECAUSE HE OR SHE WANTED TO ASK GOD FOR FORGIVENESS. WHAT A MISSED OPPORTUNITY TO HELP THE PERSON RETURN TO GOD.

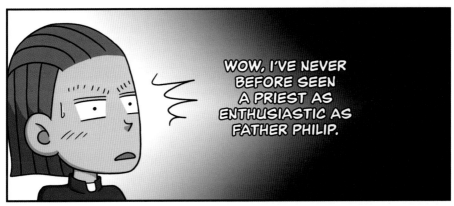

WOW, I'VE NEVER BEFORE SEEN A PRIEST AS ENTHUSIASTIC AS FATHER PHILIP.

85

YOU DIDN'T STEAL BECAUSE IT WAS FUN. YOU STOLE BECAUSE YOU WERE HUNGRY.

SAVE YOUR MONEY AND THEN PAY FOR THE BREAD YOU STOLE.

ARE YOU SURE, FATHER PHILIP, THAT GOD WILL FORGIVE ME IF I DO THAT?

YOU HAVE CONFESSED AND TOLD GOD THAT YOU ARE SORRY. WHEN I SAY THE WORDS OF ABSOLUTION, IT MEANS THAT GOD HAS FORGIVEN YOU. DO YOUR BEST NOT TO STEAL ANYMORE. WHENEVER YOU SIN, PLEASE COME SEE ME. AND . . .

I'LL WAIT AS LONG AS IT TAKES.

フサキんい ゴヌ メサイろ。

THERE'S A REALLY LONG LINE OF PEOPLE WAITING FOR CONFESSION WITH FATHER PHILIP.

YEAH, SO MANY PEOPLE ARE COMING BACK TO CHURCH NOW.

SO MANY PEOPLE WHO HAD LOST THEIR FAITH AND STOPPED COMING TO CHURCH HAVE RETURNED. THEY SAY THAT FATHER PHILIP'S WORDS DURING CONFESSION HAVE HEALED THEIR FAITH AND THEIR HEARTS.

PLEASE, BE AT PEACE AND CONFESS YOUR SINS TO GOD.

FATHER . . .

HMM, I RECOGNIZE THIS VOICE.

I DID IT AGAIN. I STOLE AGAIN.

WHAT DID YOU STEAL THIS TIME, MY SON?

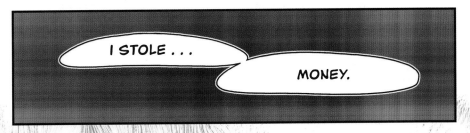

I STOLE . . .

MONEY.

I WAS GOING TO PAY THE BAKER BACK FOR THE BREAD THAT I STOLE LAST TIME. BUT SAVING ENOUGH MONEY WAS TOO HARD. I REALIZED THAT THE ONLY WAY GOD WOULD FORGIVE ME IS IF I PAID BACK THE MONEY. THAT'S WHY I STOLE MONEY FROM THE BUTCHER.

SO, YOU PAID THE BAKER FOR THE BREAD WITH MONEY YOU STOLE FROM THE BUTCHER?

YES. I LEFT THE BAKER A NOTE WITH THE MONEY FOR THE STOLEN BREAD. THE REST OF THE MONEY I KEPT.

WHAT HAPPENED AFTER THAT?

THE NEXT DAY, I USED MORE OF THE BUTCHER'S MONEY TO BUY MEAT FROM THE BUTCHER. I WAS SO NERVOUS. I THOUGHT THE BUTCHER WOULD REALIZE THAT I WAS PAYING WITH HIS MONEY. BUT HE DIDN'T—THAT MADE ME HAPPY.

HERE'S MONEY FOR THE MEAT.

OH, THANK YOU, SIR.

NOBODY LOOKED DOWN ON ME WHEN I COULD BUY BREAD AND MEAT. I LIKED THAT PEOPLE DIDN'T LOOK DOWN THEIR NOSES AT ME.

THEN I NEEDED EVEN MORE MONEY TO BUY NICE CLOTHES, AND MORE BREAD AND MEAT.

DO YOU FULLY ACKNOWLEDGE THAT WHAT YOU ARE DOING IS SINFUL?

YES, FATHER, THAT'S WHY I FEEL SO GUILTY. I'LL TRY TO NEVER DO IT AGAIN.

THEN, I CAN ABSOLVE YOU OF YOUR SINS. GOD FORGIVES YOU AND ASKS YOU NOT TO STEAL ANY MORE.

REALLY? GOD FORGIVES ME AGAIN?

OF COURSE.

GOD FORGIVES ALL PEOPLE WHO ASK HIM FOR FORGIVENESS. BUT . . .

A COUPLE OF NIGHTS LATER . . .

KNOCK KNOCK

FATHER, IT'S GETTING LATE. YOU SHOULD GO TO BED SOON.

I DON'T HAVE A WIFE WAITING FOR ME. WHAT'S THE HURRY?

OH, FATHER, STOP JOKING LIKE THAT.

BANG!

94

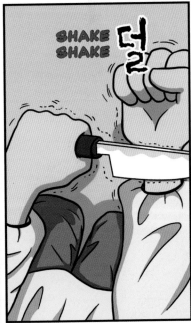

CLATTER

WEEPING

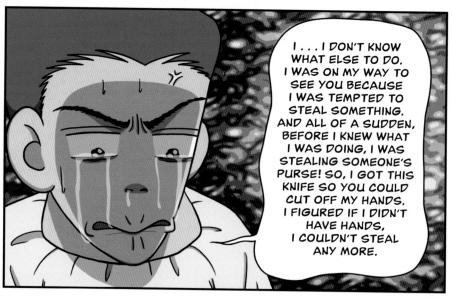

I . . . I DON'T KNOW WHAT ELSE TO DO. I WAS ON MY WAY TO SEE YOU BECAUSE I WAS TEMPTED TO STEAL SOMETHING. AND ALL OF A SUDDEN, BEFORE I KNEW WHAT I WAS DOING, I WAS STEALING SOMEONE'S PURSE! SO, I GOT THIS KNIFE SO YOU COULD CUT OFF MY HANDS. I FIGURED IF I DIDN'T HAVE HANDS, I COULDN'T STEAL ANY MORE.

I'M HOPELESS. BUT I GUESS YOU CAN'T EXPECT ANYTHING ELSE FROM A MAN LIKE ME.

99

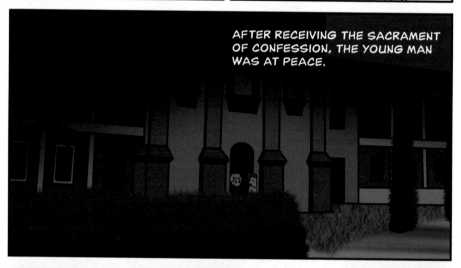

AFTER RECEIVING THE SACRAMENT OF CONFESSION, THE YOUNG MAN WAS AT PEACE.

OK, YOU KNOW WHERE TO GO.

FATHER, I'M HERE TODAY . . .

I'M DONE WITH STEALING.

I WAS ABLE TO QUIT STEALING BECAUSE YOU DIDN'T GIVE UP ON ME . . .

. . . AND YOU GUIDED ME ON THE RIGHT PATH.

COME ON, LET'S GO TO THE CONFESSIONAL.

YOU DON'T UNDERSTAND, FATHER. I HAVE NOTHING TO CONFESS TODAY.

REALLY? THAT'S GREAT. I THANK GOD EVEN MORE THAN YOU DO. ALTHOUGH, I'D GROWN USED TO SEEING YOU HERE ALL THE TIME . . .

I'LL STILL COME AROUND, BUT TO HELP OTHERS.

COME OVER AND SAY HELLO.

이쪽으로 와요

The happy birds Te Deum* sing,
'Tis Mary's month of May;
Her smile turns winter into spring,
And darkness into day;
And there's a fragrance in the air,
The bells their music make,
And oh! the world is bright and fair,
And all for Mary's sake.

Where'er we seek the holy Child,
At every sacred spot,
We meet the Mother undefiled;
Who shun her seek him not:
At cloistered Nazareth we see.
At haunted Bethlehem,
The throne of Jesus, Mary's knee,
Her smile, his diadem.

'Tis then, when at thy feet we pray,
We share our Lady's mirth;
Her joy we know who hail today
Thy Eucharistic birth;
That trembling joy to Mary sent,
Ah, Christians know it well,
With whom in his dear sacrament
Their Savior deigns to dwell.

All hail! An angel spake the words
We lovingly repeat;
The song-notes of the singing birds
They are not half so sweet:
This is a music that endures,
It cannot pass away,
For Mary's children it ensures
A never-ending May.

*TE DEUM
REFERS TO
A HYMN OF
PRAISE TO GOD.

DIOCESAN PRIESTS AND SEMINARIANS JOINED FATHER PHILIP. THROUGH SPIRITUAL CONFERENCES, GUIDED MEDITATIONS, AND PRAYERS, THESE MEN HELPED MANY PEOPLE GROW CLOSER TO GOD. FATHER PHILIP AND HIS FOLLOWERS BECAME KNOWN AS ORATORIANS, WHICH COMES FROM THE LATIN AND MEANS PEOPLE WHO PRAY.

부적 부적
CROWDED
CROWDED

바글 바글
HUGE CROWD

저기요
I CAN'T WAIT.

빼꼼
PEEK

WHAT ARE YOU LOOKING AT?

WOW, LOOK AT ALL OUR BROTHERS AND SISTERS. WHAT A HUGE CROWD.

DO YOU THINK THE POPE IS VISITING US AND THAT'S WHY THEY ALL CAME?

107

PLEASE STEP THIS WAY TO GET IN LINE.

WHIRL!

HOW DARE YOU SPEAK TO HER LIKE THAT!

MARCH

SCREECH TO A HALT

WHAT?! ARE YOU ACTUALLY GOING TO WAIT, MY LADY?!

MAXIMS AND SAYINGS OF PHILIP NERI

ONE OF THE VERY BEST MEANS OF OBTAINING HUMILITY IS SINCERE AND FREQUENT CONFESSION.

THE ORATORIANS CONTINUED TO GROW IN NUMBER, AND FATHER PHILIP WAS BUSIER THAN EVER. MANY PEOPLE ASKED HIM TO COME AND PRAY FOR THEM, AND MANY WERE MIRACULOUSLY CURED.

CROWDED

I HEARD THAT FATHER PHILIP WILL LEAD THE PRAYER MEETING TONIGHT.

YUP, THAT'S WHY WE'RE SO CROWDED.

EVEN THOUGH HE'S SO BUSY, HE STILL COMES TO PRAY WITH SIMPLE PEOPLE LIKE US. HE'S AMAZING.

HAVE YOU HEARD THE LATEST STORY?

WHAT STORY?

THE STORY ABOUT WHEN FATHER PHILIP WENT TO HELP A CHURCH OFFICIAL.

WOW, FATHER PHILIP IS ALWAYS EAGER TO HELP, ISN'T HE?

YEAH. ANYWAY, THE CHURCH OFFICIAL WAS SO SICK, THEY CALLED FATHER PHILIP BECAUSE PHILIP HAS CURED MANY PEOPLE.

112

FATHER PHILIP WENT TO SEE HIM AND LISTENED TO HIS CONFESSION. THEN FATHER PHILIP PRAYED OVER HIM.

AFTER A COUPLE OF DAYS . . .

THE GUY'S LEGS, WHICH HAD BEEN BADLY INFECTED, WERE HEALED!

IT'S A MIRACLE!

I CAN HARDLY BELIEVE IT!

I THOUGHT EVERYONE KNEW THAT STORY.

GOOD EVENING, EVERYONE. LET'S BEGIN OUR PRAYER.

LATER THAT EVENING . . .

OK, EVERYONE, WE'LL MEET AGAIN NEXT WEEK.

FATHER, BECAUSE OF YOUR PREDICTION, I WAS ABLE TO AVOID GETTING INTO AN ACCIDENT.

HAHA. PRAISE GOD THAT YOU WEREN'T HURT.

FATHER, COULD YOU BLESS MY BABY?

FATHER PHILIP!

FATHER, ARE YOU JESUS? PLEASE BLESS ME. IF YOU TOUCH ME AND BLESS ME, MAYBE I'LL BE ABLE TO BE LIKE YOU.

AN OLD MAN? PLUS, MY CHILD, I'M NOT JESUS.

116

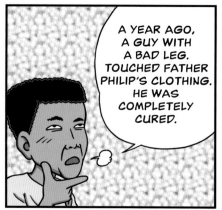

A YEAR AGO, A GUY WITH A BAD LEG, TOUCHED FATHER PHILIP'S CLOTHING. HE WAS COMPLETELY CURED.

AND FATHER PHILIP TOLD ME NOT TO GO TO THE BEACH BECAUSE I WOULD GET HURT. I DIDN'T GO AND I AVOIDED AN ACCIDENT. FATHER PHILIP CAN PREDICT THE FUTURE.

FATHER!!! CURE ME!

STOP AT ONCE OR YOU'LL BE VERY SORRY!

PLEASE, LET ME TOUCH YOUR CLOTHES.

신부님

저도—

머리카락 한 올만—

옷자락 한 번만—

JUST TOUCH MY HEAD ONE TIME.

PHHHRRT

EWWW!

WHAT'S THAT SMELL?!

1577 AT
SAN GIROLAMO

FATHER, MAY I ASK YOU A QUESTION?

OF COURSE. ASK ME ANYTHING.

(HE HAS QUITE A THICK ACCENT . . . INTERESTING.)

TODAY IS SUNDAY, BUT ALL THE PRIESTS SEEM TO HAVE SOMEWHERE IMPORTANT TO GO. IT DOESN'T LOOK LIKE THEY'RE GOING TO VISIT FAMILY. AND I'VE NOTICED THAT MOST OF THEM EVEN GO OUT LATE AT NIGHT DURING THE WEEK.

ARE THEY ALL GETTING TOGETHER TO GO PRAY SOMEWHERE . . .

OR . . .

ARE THEY GOING OUT TO EAT DELICIOUS ITALIAN FOOD BUT NOT INVITING ME BECAUSE I'M A FOREIGNER?

YUP. THE SECOND ONE!

KIDDING KIDDING.

PHILIP AND HIS JOKES ARE A BAD INFLUENCE. HEE HEE

ALL THE PRIESTS GO TO THE "ORATORY."

WHAT'S THE ORATORY?

YOU HAVEN'T BEEN HERE TOO LONG. THAT'S WHY YOU HAVEN'T HEARD ABOUT IT.

123

HAVE YOU HEARD ABOUT FATHER PHILIP NERI?

YES. I HEARD HE'S A GREAT PRIEST WITH A WONDERFUL SENSE OF HUMOR. I HEAR EVERYONE RESPECTS HIM.

ALL OF THAT IS TRUE. WHAT YOU MAY NOT HAVE HEARD IS THAT HE FOUNDED A GROUP OF PRIESTS. THEY MEET REGULARLY FOR SPIRITUAL GROWTH AND LISTEN TO EACH OTHERS CONFESSIONS.

THAT GROUP IS KNOWN AS THE CONGREGATION OF THE ORATORY.

PRIESTS MEETING IN SOME BUILDING INSTEAD OF A CHURCH? IT'S UNUSUAL . . .

PLEASE, BROTHERS, DON'T BE SHY. I'D LOVE TO BE YOUR CONFESSOR.

IT STARTED AS A SMALL GROUP MEETING IN A HALL . . .

THANK YOU, FATHER PHILIP.

FATHER, DO YOU HAVE TIME TO HEAR MY CONFESSION?

FATHER, I WAS HOPING YOU WOULD PRAY WITH ME.

BUT IT GREW AND GREW. SO MANY PRIESTS ARE GATHERING THERE AND THEY WANT TO PRAY AND GO TO CONFESSION.

YES, OF COURSE!

WE ARE SO CROWDED! HAHAHA

MOBBED

OVER THE LAST SEVERAL YEARS, THE ORATORIANS HAVE REALLY GROWN IN NUMBER.

125

THESE PRIESTS AND LAYMEN DON'T TAKE VOWS* BUT THEY PRAY TOGETHER AND SUPPORT ONE ANOTHER IN THEIR COMMON MISSION OF SERVING GOD'S PEOPLE. THEY PRAY, SING, AND READ FROM SCRIPTURE AND THE WRITINGS OF THE CHURCH FATHERS AND THE MARTYRS.

THEN THEY MINISTER TO GOD'S PEOPLE BY FINDING VARIOUS WAYS OF PROCLAIMING THE GOOD NEWS TO THEM. THE PEOPLE TOO COME FOR SPIRITUAL CONFERENCES AND CONFESSION. IT'S AMAZING TO SEE ALL WE DO.

*PRIESTS WHO BELONG TO RELIGIOUS ORDERS (LIKE THE FRANCISCANS, JESUITS, AND DOMINICANS) TAKE VOWS OF POVERTY, CHASTITY, AND OBEDIENCE.

A FEW YEARS AGO ON JULY 15, 1575, POPE GREGORY XIII GAVE US HIS APPROVAL WHEN HE GAVE US THE CHURCH OF SANTA MARIA IN VALLICELLA. THE ORATORIANS MEET THERE.

SOUNDS LIKE . . .

THEY'RE GREAT!

HOW IS FATHER PHILIP?

SHUT

HE'S CONSCIOUS NOW, BUT . . .

HE'S WEAK, OVERWORKED AND MALNOURISHED, WHICH HAS CAUSED THIS FEVER TO REALLY TAKE A TOLL ON HIM.

WE HAD NO IDEA. HE MUST HAVE BEEN SO BUSY TAKING CARE OF EVERYONE ELSE THAT HE HASN'T BEEN TAKING CARE OF HIMSELF.

NOW THAT WE KNOW, WE CAN MAKE HIM TAKE CARE OF HIMSELF.

GRRRRR

MART—

WHY? WHAT?

YOU'RE ALWAYS A LITTLE MEAN TO ME. NOW I KNOW YOU REALLY CARE ABOUT ME. YOU'RE WORRIED, HUH?

WHATEVER! I'M NOT WORRIED!

MARTINO, I'M FINE NOW.

GOD IS GIVING ME THIS TIME TO REST. I STILL HAVE A FEW YEARS BEFORE I MEET HIM FACE-TO-FACE. SO DON'T WORRY.

OVER THE NEXT SEVERAL YEARS PHILIP WOULD SUFFER FROM SERIOUS ILLNESSES AND RECOVER ONLY TO FALL SICK AGAIN.

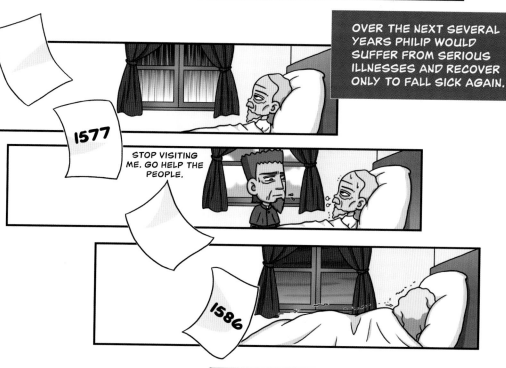

1594

1595

SO, HOW IS HE THIS TIME? IS HE GETTING BETTER?

NO.

HE CAN'T GET BETTER BECAUSE HE REFUSES TO TAKE ANY MEDICINE. I HAVE NO IDEA HOW HE IS STILL ALIVE.

HE'S ALIVE BECAUSE OF THE GREAT FAITH HE HAS. IT'S KIND OF MOVING, ACTUALLY.

MAY 1595

WHEEZE

GROAN

UHHH . . .

JUDGING BY ALL HIS GROANS, FATHER PHILIP MUST BE IN SO MUCH PAIN. HE'S USUALLY JOKING AND CHEERFUL, BUT LATELY HE CAN'T CONTAIN THE PAIN.

I'VE HEARD PEOPLE SAY THAT SAINTS OFTEN SUFFER A LOT BEFORE GOING TO HEAVEN. MAYBE HE'LL GO TO HEAVEN SOON.

GLARE
찌릿

늘췄!
GASP

늘췄!
GASP

FATHER, THE BODY OF CHRIST.

하...
하
MOAN....

AMEN. THANK YOU, LORD.

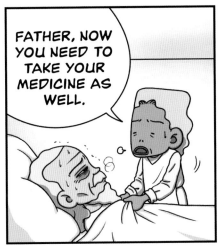

143

OH, MY JESUS . . .

FORGIVE ME AND LET ME SEE YOU IN HEAVEN SOON.

MAXIMS AND SAYINGS OF PHILIP NERI

OUR SWEET JESUS, THROUGH THE EXCESS OF HIS LOVE AND KINDNESS, HAS LEFT HIMSELF TO US IN THE MOST HOLY SACRAMENT.

FATHER PHILIP HAS BEEN SICK FOR SO LONG. ONE DAY HE SEEMS FINE AND BACK TO HIS JOKING SELF, AND ABLE TO CELEBRATE MASS. THEN THE NEXT DAY HE'S SERIOUSLY ILL.

HE'S NOT GETTING BETTER. WE CAN'T JUST SIT BACK AND WATCH HIM WASTE AWAY. ISN'T THERE ANYTHING WE CAN DO?

YOU KNOW, PHILIP ONCE TOLD ME THAT HE HAD RESERVED MAY 26, 1595 AS THE DAY HE WOULD GO TO GOD.

146

THAT'S PRETTY PRECISE, MAY 26, 1595 . . .

I NEVER REALLY KNEW IF HE WAS JOKING OR NOT. BUT MAYBE IT WAS ONE OF HIS MANY PREDICTIONS.

WELL, I GUESS WE'LL KNOW SOON ENOUGH. IT IS MAY 1595 . . .

AND YESTERDAY WAS THE 25TH . . . SO THE 26TH IS . . .

FATHER! FATHER MARTINO!!

TODAY!!

147

151

152

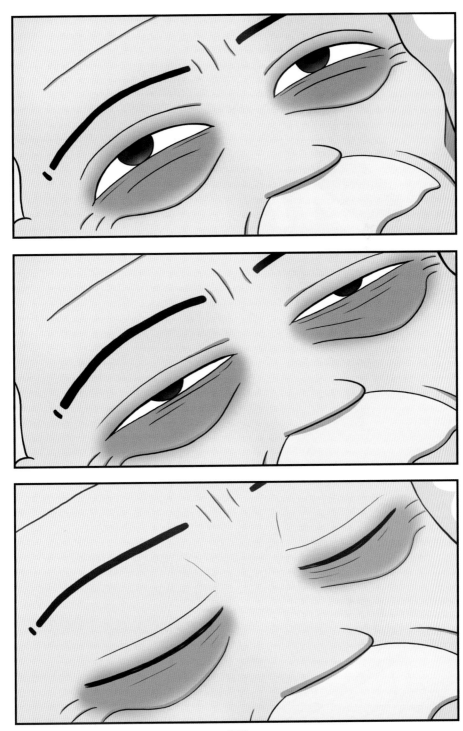

CLANG

CLANG

FATHER PHILIP NERI
HAS PASSED AWAY. HE IS NOW
WITH GOD!

DON'T BE SAD, MY FRIENDS.
I HAD A GREAT TIME WITH YOU.

I'M SO HAPPY
THAT I COULD
BE OF SOME
HELP, EVEN
THOUGH WHAT
I DID WAS
LITTLE.

HEY YOU, THAT
BOWL IS TOO BIG!

PLEASE COME AND LET ME
SERVE YOU. THIS SOUP IS
SO GOOD.

THANK
YOU!

IF YOU ARE UNWELL, PLEASE COME TO THE CHURCH.

HEY, YOUNG MAN, WILL YOU TAKE ME TO THE CHURCH?

WHAT'S THAT ON MY CHEST? SOMEONE LEFT ME BREAD!

I REJOICED WHEN YOU OPENED YOUR HEART TO GOD.

FATHER, DO YOU HAVE TIME TO HEAR MY CONFESSION?

YES, OF COURSE!

FATHER, I WAS HOPING YOU WOULD PRAY WITH ME.

I WAS SO HAPPY AND BLESSED TO BE AMONG YOU.

158

THE MAXIMS AND SAYINGS OF SAINT PHILIP NERI

LET THE YOUNG BE CHEERFUL, AND INDULGE IN THE RECREATIONS PROPER TO THEIR AGE, PROVIDED THEY KEEP OUT OF THE WAY OF SIN.

DEVOTION TO THE BLESSED VIRGIN IS ACTUALLY NECESSARY, BECAUSE THERE IS NO BETTER MEANS OF OBTAINING GOD'S GRACES THAN THROUGH HIS MOST HOLY MOTHER.

IF THE YOUNG WISH TO PRESERVE THEIR PURITY, LET THEM AVOID BAD COMPANY.

THE TRUE WAY TO ADVANCE IN HOLY VIRTUES IS TO PERSEVERE IN A HOLY CHEERFULNESS.

A MOST EXCELLENT MEANS OF KEEPING OURSELVES PURE IS TO LAY OPEN ALL OUR THOUGHTS, AS SOON AS POSSIBLE, TO OUR CONFESSOR WITH THE GREATEST SINCERITY, AND KEEP NOTHING HIDDEN IN OURSELVES.

THE CHEERFUL ARE MUCH EASIER TO GUIDE IN THE SPIRITUAL LIFE THAN THE MELANCHOLY.

THE NAME OF JESUS, PRONOUNCED WITH REVERENCE AND AFFECTION, HAS A KIND OF POWER TO SOFTEN THE HEART.

AT COMMUNION WE OUGHT TO ASK FOR THE REMEDY OF THE VICE TO WHICH WE FEEL OURSELVES MOST INCLINED.

BE DEVOUT TO THE MADONNA, KEEP YOURSELF FROM SIN, AND GOD WILL DELIVER YOU FROM YOUR EVILS.

HUMAN LANGUAGE CANNOT EXPRESS THE BEAUTY OF A SOUL THAT DIES IN A STATE OF GRACE.

NOTHING HELPS A PERSON MORE THAN PRAYER.

IN ORDER TO PRESERVE THEIR PURITY, PEOPLE SHOULD FREQUENT THE SACRAMENTS, AND ESPECIALLY CONFESSION.

WE MUST AVOID LIES AS WE WOULD A PESTILENCE.

IF GOD BE WITH US, THERE IS NOTHING ELSE TO FEAR.